—— THE ——
ANGLER'S
GUIDE

Unicorn Press Ltd
66 Charlotte Street
London
W1T 4QE

www.unicornpress.org

Published by Unicorn Press Ltd 2015

ISBN 978-19100-65464

10 9 8 7 6 5 4 3 2 1

Cover designed by Felicity Price-Smith
Typeset and printed in India by Imprint Digital.

T. F. SALTER

—— THE ——
ANGLER'S GUIDE

ILLUSTRATIONS BY THE AUTHOR

Unicorn Press Ltd

CONTENTS.

Page

PREFACE.

CLAPTON, *August*, 1816.

FINDING myself unable to enjoy the pleasure of angling so frequently as I have been accustomed to do, (in consequence of declining health) I have employed some of my leisure time in writing this work as a Guide to the young and inexperienced angler. The information it contains, is the result of more than forty years practice and experience; it will be seen that I have recommended the angler to use fine tackle, small hooks, &c. and to depend more on skill than strength, (generally speaking) being fully convinced that in so doing, though he may sustain some loss, he will have much gain. I admit, that in some waters where fish much abound and are seldom disturbed, great execution may be done with coarse tackle, also while the waters are thick or coloured, and in the spring, while the Roach, Dace, &c. are on the shallows spawning; at such times a gut line may do, nearly as well as one made of single hair, a No. 10 hook as well as a No. 12, &c. The Author thinks it proper here to state, that his motive for publishing this Abridgement of his Angler's Guide, (for a character, &c. of which work, see the back cover of this Book) is to enable the fishing-tackle dealers to sell at a small price to the novice in angling, a work of real practical Information on the Art of taking Fish.

THE
ANGLER'S PROGRESS.

WHEN I was a mere school-boy (ere yet I'd learn'd my book),
I felt a wish for augling in every little brook:
With osier-rod, some thread for line, a crooked pin for hook,
Of Pricklebacks and Minnows each day I caught a store,
With Stone Loaches and Miller's Thumbs, those brooks afford
    no more.

Then next I bought some farthing hooks, and eke a horse-hair
    line,
A hazel rod with whalebone top, my playmates to outshine;
With which I soon aspir'd to angle with a float,
And where I could not fish from shore, I angl'd from a boat.
Then Roach and Dace, and Bleak, I took, and Gudgeons with-
    out end,
And now and then a Perch I'd hook, which made my rod to
    bend;
And thus the little angler (pleas'd with his line and hook)
Would shun each noisy wrangler to fish the murm'ring brook.

Bream, Chub, and Barbel, next I sought, their various haunts
    I try'd,
With scower'd worms, cheese-paste, and greaves, and various
    baits beside,
With hooks of Kirby bent, (well chose) and gut that's round
    and fine,
So by gradations thus I rose, to fish with running-line:
A multiplying-winch I bought, wherewith my skill to try,
And so expert myself I thought, few with me now could vie—
And thus the little angler, with rod and line, and hook,
Would shun each noisy wrangler to fish the murm'ring brook.

My mind on Trolling now intent, with live or dead snap hook,
And seldom to the rivers went, but Pike or Jack I took:
Near banks of bullrush, sedge and reed, (a dark and windy
    day)
And if the Pike were on the feed, I rarely miss'd my prey.
If baits are fresh and proper size, no matter what's the sort,
At Gudgeons, Roach or Dace, (they'll rise with all by turns),
    I've sport.
So now a dext'rous angler, with rod and line, and hook,
I shun each noisy wrangler to fish the murm'ring brook.

And now to cast a fly-line well, became my chiefest wish,
I strove each sportsman to excel, and cheat the nimble fish:
Now Trout and Grayling I could kill, (if gloomy was the day)
And Salmon also, (at my will) became an easy prey.
Now flies and palmers I would dress; aquatic insects too,
And all their various seasons guess, their uses well I knew.
So now the perfect angler, with rod and line, and hook,
I shun each noisy wrangler to fish the murm'ring brook.

Songs of the Chace.

LIST OF HOOKS.

The following list of hooks to be used in the rivers Thames and Lea, will prevent the trouble of referring to the different chapters:

For Barbel fishing in the Thames, . . Nos. 6, 7, and 8 Hook.
For Barbel fishing in the Lea, ... Nos.   8 and 9 Hook.
For Gudgeon fishing in the Thames, . . Nos. 10 and 11 Hook.
For Gudgeon fishing in the Lea, . . . Nos. 11 and 12 Hook.
For Perch fishing, ... Nos.   7 and 8 Hook.
For Carp fishing, ... Nos.   9 and 10 Hook.
For Roach, Dace, and Bleak, ... Nos. 11, 12, 13 Hook.

The above sizes are such as the best anglers of the present day always prefer, and are much smaller than those which were commonly used thirty years since. At that time larger hooks and stronger tackle might have been used with success; but, unfortunately for the lovers of angling, the stock of fish in most rivers has been gradually on the decline, and the number being smaller, they are consequently better supplied with food, and are therefore more cautious of risking their lives when strong tackle and large hooks are offered. The angler who expects success, therefore, must adopt the modern tackle, or he will not fail to be disappointed. It is true a few Roach, Dace, Gudgeons, &c. may be taken with a twisted hair line, cork float, and No. 8 or 9 hook; but to have reasonable chance for good sport, the old heavy tackle must be exploded, and in its place the fine light rods, lines and float, and as small a hook as the nature of the water will allow of must be adopted, and what is wanting in strength of tackle the angler must supply in skill.

JANUARY.

The only fish that will take a bait this month are Jark, Pike, Chub and Roach, for which you may angle an hour or two in the middle of the day, provided the water is sufficiently clear.

FEBRUARY.

In the latter end of February, if the weather is mild for the season, Carp, Perch, Roach and Chub, as well as Jack and Pike will feed: they all prefer live baits at this season. Fish only in the middle of the day, and in eddies near the banks, for fish always get to the scowers and shallows, and near the banks after winter, and remain there till after they have spawned.

MARCH.

During this month Jack, Pike, Carp, Perch, Roach, Dace, Chub, Gudgeon, and Minnows will take a bait: still continue to use a live bait generally, and prefer the middle of the day. Angle in the shallows and eddies near the banks. Jack, Pike, Smelts, Flounders, Bleak and Perch, spawn in this month.

APRIL.

All the fish enumerated in March, with the addition of Trout, will feed this month, and sometimes

Tench (in rivers;) also Barbel, Bleak, Flounders and Eels—bait as before. Angle in shallows, sharps, &c. as in March. Barbel, Dace, Gudgeons, Minnows, Rudd, Bream, and Pope or Ruff, spawn this month.

MAY.

During this month Eels will run and take a bait night and day, and all the different species of fresh-water fish now feed and take baits at top and bottom of the water; also in ponds, you may expect sport. Still prefer to angle in the shallows, sharps, streams and eddies. Roach, Chub, Carp, Miller's Thumb, and Umber or Grayling, spawn this month.

JUNE.

This month the angler will find but indifferent sport, most fish have recently spawned, and are out of condition, except Trout, which are now healthy and strong. Angle in the streams, eddies and currents. Tench spawn this month.

JULY.

All fresh-water fish will now feed, but best in the morning and evening, and will take a variety of baits; but from the quantity of food they get from weeds, and not having quite recovered from spawning, they will not take a bait freely: still continue to angle in the streams and scowers. Gudgeons spawn again this month.

AUGUST.

All kinds of fish will take a bait more freely than last month, but best very early, and late in the evening: prefer the stream during this month for angling. Carp and Smelts spawn again this month.

SEPTEMBER.

This month is a good season for most kinds of angling, from early in the morning till late at night. Barbel, Chub, Roach and Dace, are now leaving the weeds, and get into deep water.

OCTOBER.

This month is good for trolling and bottom fishing for Roach and Chub, but not for fly-fishing, or angling in ponds or still waters. The weeds are now sour and rotten, and the fish are all in holes and deep water.

NOVEMBER.

Chub, Roach, Jack and Pike will still feed, and sometimes freely in the middle of the day.

DECEMBER.

Chub, Roach, Jack and Pike continue to afford the angler amusement and profit, if a favourable opportunity offers to exercise his skill, which seldom occurs this month, as the waters are generally too thick, or frozen up. Barbel, Carp, and Gudgeons are now retired to their winter quarters, the Eels are also buried in numbers together deep in holes or mud.

> The fields their verdure now resign,
> The bleating flocks and lowing kine,
>   Give o'er their former play:
> The feather'd tribe forgets the notes
> Which joyful strain'd their vocal throats,
>   To chaunt the matin lay.

———

A

L I S T

OF THE

PRINCIPAL RIVERS IN ENGLAND,

WITH THE

VARIOUS KIND OF FISH WHICH THEY CONTAIN.

The rivers Thames and Lea, with some others of note, are thus comprehended in one of Mr. Drayton's sonnets:

> Our floods queen Thames, for ships and swans is crown'd,
> And stately Severn for her shore is prais'd;
> The crystal Trent for fords and fish renown'd,
> And Avon's fame to Albion's cliffs is rais'd:

Carlegion Chester vaunts her holy Dee,
York many wonders of her Ouse can tell;
The Peak her Dove, whose banks so fertile be,
And Kent will say her Medway does excel;
Gotswold commends her Isis to the Tame;
Our northern borders boast of Tweed's fair flood;
Our western parts extol their Willy's fame,
And the old Lea brags of the Danish blood.

The Rivers Severn, Trent, Dove, Medway, &c
DESCRIBED.

There are more than three hundred rivers in England and Wales; I shall describe the course of some of the most considerable, and notice the fish in them with which they most abound.

SEVERN.

This river takes its rise in Montgomeryshire in Wales, and runs through part of Shropshire, Staffordshire, and Worcestershire, passing below Worcester, and runs on to the city of Gloucester. This river abounds with Salmon, Trout, Eels, and other fish.

TRENT.

This river first shows itself in Staffordshire, and in its course it passes Nottingham, Newark and Hull to Gainsborough. It now loses its name by mixing in the Humber, which falls into the sea at Flamborough Head. This is a noble river, and well stocked with Jack, Carp, Eels, Barbel, Chub,

Perch, Roach, Flounders, &c. many small rivers help to supply the Trent during its course; all well stored with Trout, namely, the Dove, the Sour, the Idle, the Leen, &c.

DOVE.

This river rises near the three Shire stones in Derbyshire, passes on to Ashbourn, from thence falls into the Trent. This little river abounds with Trout and also Grayling.

MEDWAY.

This river rises in Sussex, through which county and Kent it flows to Rochester and Chatham, passing by Maidstone, &c. and is well stored with Salmon and other fish.

STOUR.

This river rises in Kent, runs past Ashford round Canterbury, from thence to Hackington, Forditch, and continues its course to Sandwich, and there empties itself into the sea. This river abounds with Trout.

OUSE.

This river rises in Oxfordshire, proceeds to Buckinham, gliding on to Bedford and Huntington, from thence to Ely, and falls into the sea at Lynn in Norfolk. The Ouse is well stored with Jack, Pike, Perch, Eels, &c.

CAM.

This river rises in Cambridgeshire, runs by Cambridge, and after some miles is lost in the river

Ouse. The Cam does not boast of Trout, but it may of Jack, Pike, Carp, Perch, Eels, Roach, &c. There are many large pieces of water near this river, known by the names of Meers, Lakes, &c. full of fine Tench and various other fish; also in Rumsey-mere, near Huntingdon, famous for Eels and Pike.

TAMER

This river divides the counties of Cornwall and Devonshire, passes Launceston, Saltash, and Plymouth Dock, and falls into Plymouth Sound. This river contains more Salmon than any other in the West of England.

EX.

This river rises in Somersetshire, passes Tiverton and Exeter, and empties itself in the sea at Exmouth; during its course it takes the waters of several streams, and is well stored with Salmon, Trout, Eels, &c.

ITCHIN.

This river rises in Hampshire, and passes by Rumsey and Winchester, and falls into the sea at Southampton. This river abounds with Salmon and Trout.

WYE.

This river rises in Montgomeryshire, passes by Hereford and Monmouth, and falls into the Severn below Chepstow. This river is stowed with Trout and Grayling.

THE

ANGLER'S GUIDE.

CHAP. I.

ON THE CHOICE OF TACKLE—HOW TO FASTEN THE LINE TO THE ROD—TO PLUMB THE DEPTH—TO BAIT THE HOOK, &c.

IN the following treatise it is not my intention to take up the time of my readers by instructing them how to make fish-ponds, angle-rods, floats, or lines, conceiving that such descriptions tend only to perplex and confuse the young angler; but shall direct him in the choice of every necessary article used in angling, which may at all times be purchased at the principal fishing-tackle shops in London.

The angle-rod is a material article in the angler's catalogue, therefore much care should be taken to procure a good one: the shops keep a great variety, made of bamboo, cane, hazel, hickery, &c. and of different lengths, some fitted as walking canes,

B

and others to pack in canvas bags; the latter are to be preferred, because you may have them of any length, and they are generally made more true, and are stronger; those made of bamboo are best for general fishing, having several tops of various strengths, but the rods made of cane are much superior for fine fishing, particularly for Roach. In choosing a rod, observe that it is perfectly strait when all the joints are put together, and that it gradually tapers from the butt to the top. In the choice of lines, take those that are round and even, whether made of gut or horse-hair: in respect to colour, I think sorrel best for single horse-hair, either as a line or tied on a hook.

Floats for fine fishing should be made of quill, some are called tip-cap'd, which are best for roach fishing, others have a plug at bottom, and are called plug floats; several other kinds are used, made of quill and cork, called cork floats, others of the porcupine quill, &c.

In purchasing a winch, give the preference to a multiplying one, as it enables you to lengthen or shorten your line with facility, by which means you much sooner kill your fish: those which tie on the rod are better than those made with a ring or hoop, as they can be fastened on either large or small joints—not so with the ring'd.

The following is a list of articles necessary for every one to possess, who intends perfecting himself in the delightful art of angling.

Rods for trolling, and bottom-fishing;

Lines of gut, hair, &c. (those of three yards long will be found most useful)

Floats of various sizes, to suit any water;

Hooks for trolling,—the gorge, snap, &c. tied on gymp;

Hooks, tied on gut, of various sizes, to No. 12;

Hooks, tied on hair, from No. 11 to 13;

Winches for running tackle;

Plummets for taking the depth;

Baiting needle;

Disgorger;

Clearing ring;

Drag;

Split Shot;

Caps for floats;

Landing net;

Kettle for carrying live bait;

Gentle boxes;

Bags for worms;

Fly-fishing rods, for whipping and dapping, or dabbing;

Book or case of artificial flies, moths, &c. and materials for making the same.

When you fasten the line to the rod, pass the loop of your line through the ring at the extremity of the top joint of your rod and carry it over the ferril, and then draw your line up to the top again, the loop will then be fast and the line will hang from the ring at the extreme point of the rod. To

plumb the depth take a folding plummet and un-
fold about two inches of it, put your hook over its
side, then fold the plummet up again, which prevents the hook slipping off; now cast in your line,
and when the plummet is on the ground and the
tip of the float just appears above the water, you
have the right depth for fishing at bottom. When
you bait your hook with a worm, enter the point of
the hook in the worm a little below its head and
carry it down near to the tail; when you bait with
paste use a piece the size of a small pea.

CHAP. II.

TROLLING FOR JACK AND PIKE; IN WHAT WATERS
THEY ABOUND MOST, AND HOW TO TAKE
THEM; ALSO HOW TO BAIT THE HOOKS WITH
LIVE AND DEAD BAITS.

THE Jack and Pike, are well known to be the
tyrants of rivers, lakes, and ponds, but they afford
the angler much amusement, sport, and exercise
in trolling for them, and they are also held in
much estimation at table, being considered as one
of the best fish the fresh waters produce; they are
therfore sought after with the greatest avidity by

the angler, and every art and stratagem is employed to take them: these I shall fully detail to my readers, but will first acquaint them where those fish are most abundant, and then proceed to take or kill *secundum artem.*

The rivers Thames and Lea probably breed a greater variety of fish than any other rivers in England, and among the various species, a good store of Jack and Pike; yet the angler will find but few places in the Thames within twenty miles of London, likely to reward him for his skill or assiduity in trolling: this is chiefly arising from the rapidity of the stream, and the few still holes or eddies to be met with on its banks. The places nearest to London where I have met with any success, are from the meadows at Isleworth, proceeding to Richmond-bridge; thence to Twickenham, and again from the banks at Teddington to Hampton-wick; also at Hampton, Moulesey-hurst, at and near Esher, Walton, Sunbury, and on to Chertsey-bridge. During this route the troller may find likely places on both sides of the river.

The river Lea abounds with Jack and Pike; its numerous creeks, bends, pools, tumbling-bays, &c. give much security and harbour for fish; a great many parts of it also are secured from poachers, by being rented and preserved for the sole purpose of angling: these are called subscription waters, which the angler may use at his pleasure, by paying annually a certain sum, in no case exceeding twenty-one shillings.

At a distance of less than three miles from the metropolis, the angler will find many excellent places for trolling in this river, which, for thirty miles up, is not generally more than thirty yards broad, enabling the experienced angler to fish its whole breadth from one side, in many parts for a mile together, without interruption. The little navigable river Stort, which runs into the Lea near the Rye-house, Hoddesden, contains many Jack and Pike. The river Roding, in Essex, is well stored with fine Jack and Pike at Ongar; and also at Aibridge, Loughton, Woodford-bridge, and in several holes in the fields between Woodford-bridge and Red-bridge, at the back of Wanstead, and from thence to Ilford and Barking-creek.

At Dagenham in Essex, the large piece of water called Dagenham-breach (which is preserved for the use of subscribers) has very large and numerous Jack and Pike. The Camberwell canal will repay the angler for trolling, as he will meet with some good Jack and Pike in it, particularly in that part of the canal which is broad and deep near the bridge or arch on the Kent-road, on the east side, all the way to Deptford Lower-road. The Croydon canal also boasts of some Jack, which may be trolled for from Deptford to Croydon, particularly in the still waters belonging to the numerous locks between New Cross, Kent-road, (to the east of

Nunhead-hill,) and Sydenham. I have taken several Jack and Pike in the Paddington canal; the best place is close to the first brick bridge from Paddington, on the west side. Jack and Pike are also to be met with in several other waters near London, but I have had the greatest success trolling in those rivers and canals above mentioned.

The natural baits for Jack and Pike are Roach, Dace, Gudgeon, Bleak, and Chub: about six or seven inches in length will be found the best size, though some anglers use them considerably larger; but I have not found my account in trolling with a large bait: for by experience I have noticed the Jack or Pike to be sometimes shy of pouching, holding it across their mouths a considerable time, swimming backwards and forwards, and at last dropping it, while, on the contrary, they will generally pouch a small lively bait in a few minutes. Another advantage also often results from using a small bait—you may take a Trout, Perch, or Chub with it; the two latter are frequently taken when trolling for Jack or Pike, particularly if you have a live Gudgeon on your hook. The Roach, Dace, and Gudgeon are decidedly the best baits for Jack or Pike; the Bleak may be used in thick water, because it is a very bright fish, but it is too thin to look well on the hook, and very soon loses its scales: small Chub and Perch, with the back fin cut off, are used when no better can be met with. The shops keep artificial baits for trolling, both of fish and frogs, made of wood, pearl, and also of leather stuffed and painted, and which, in form and colour, much resemble nature, but I should never think of using them while there was a possibility of getting a natural one: when they are used, it is with the snap, which I think shows judgment, for surely the most sanguine angler could hardly expect a Pike to pouch either wood, pearl, or leather even with the addition of stuffing.

There are several methods practised in trolling and fishing for Jack and Pike, but the following are generally used, namely, with the gorge, the snap, the live bait, and the bead hook.

The gorge hook is loaded on the shank with lead, and introduced into the body of the bait; the snap hook, either spring or dead snap, consists of three hooks fastened together, and are put on the bait without entering the body: the hooks used for live bait are single or double.—I always use the single.

To bait these hooks observe the following directions: first the gorge hook.—Take a baiting needle, and hook the curved end of it to the loop of the gymp, (to which the hook is tied) then introduce the point of the needle into the bait's mouth, and bring it out at the tail, the lead will then be hid in the bait's belly, and the points and barbs will lie in its mouth, the points turning upwards: to keep the bait steady on the hook, tie the tail-part to the gymp with some white thread. The advantages arising from the use of the gorge hook is principally from the hook lying so much within the bait's mouth, and the gymp coming from the tail, which prevents every obstruction to pouching: this is not the case with any other baited hook; for it is to be observed, that the Jack or Pike, in pouching, always swallows the bait head foremost.

The spring snap hook is baited by introducing the point of the upper or small hook under the skin of the bait on the side, and bringing it up to the back fin.

The dead snap is baited by the loop of the gymp being passed inside the gill of the bait, and brought out at the mouth; the lead lies in the throat, the first hook outside the gill, and the others on its side, with the points just entered under the skin. It is best to sew this bait's mouth up with some white thread, to keep the lead and hooks in their places.

The live bait is simply passing the hook through the bait's lips, or the flesh beneath the back fin, taking care not to wound the back bone, or the bait will soon die.

The bead hook is formed of two single hooks tied back to back, or you may purchase them made of one piece of wire tied to gymp; between the lower part of the shanks is fastened a small link or two of chains, having a piece of lead of a conical form, or like a drop bead, (from which it takes its name) linked by a staple to it: the lead is put into the live bait's mouth, (a Gudgeon is the best bait) which is sewed up with white thread.

Angling with this bait is called live bait trolling, for when you angle with a live bait, and have a float on the line, you wait some time in a place while the bait swims about, consequently not much ground is travelled over or length of water fished in a day, therefore not intitled to the name of trolling.

Trolling is derived from the French word *troller*, to stroll or rove about, which is the case frequently when angling with the gorge or snap, to the distance of eight or ten miles up a river and back again, trolling forwards and backwards, as you then carry the baits in your pocket; but in live bait angling or trolling, you are encumbered with a fish kettle.

The lines for trolling are made of silk, and silk twisted with hair or gut: the platted silk is the best line, which should be kept on the winch in length from thirty to forty yards at least, I have known a pike to run out near a hundred yards of line in Dagenham Breach.

The rod used in trolling must be very strong, with a stiff whalebone or hickery top. I find a rod made in the following manner very portable: let the butt be something more than a yard long, and of sufficient thickness to admit two stout joints; the top made of hickery, about eighteen inches in length, which I commonly carry in my inside coat pocket, the other joints forming a good walking cane, and with a bait or two in my pocket, I pass without any one suspecting that I am going on a fishing excursion: this rod, when put together, will measure about fourteen feet, which I find generally long enough for trolling in any water.

Having described the way to bait the hooks, &c. we will now repair to the river, and learn how to cast a bait, and kill either Jack or Pike. In the frontispiece the reader will see the different modes of baiting hooks for trolling, with the exception of the bead hook, which is given below.

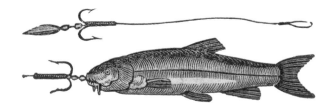

CHAP. III.

TROLLING CONCLUDED; HOW TO CAST THE BAIT AND KILL JACK OR PIKE.

I SHALL suppose the young angler to have arrived at the river side with his rod and line, and a gorge hook baited. First fasten the winch to the butt of the rod, draw the line through the rings to the length of eight or ten yards, and fasten the hook on the line with a small swivel; place the bottom of the butt against the side of your stomach, draw some of the line back with your left hand, and lower the top of the rod near the ground, then with a jerk from your right arm cast the bait into the water: while giving the jerk, keep the butt firm against your stomach, but let the line, which you hold in the left hand, loose. By a little practice, the young angler may be able to cast his bait to any distance; but if the river or piece of water is not very large, or when it is proper to cast your bait near the bank or shore, it is then only necessary to hold the rod in your right hand instead of placing it against your stomach, and holding the line as before directed in the left hand, you may with much ease cast the bait to the place you think most likely to find a Jack, this is properly termed dipping. When you cast in the bait, let it fall on the water as lightly as you can, that the fish may not be alarmed by the water being much agitated; let it sink to the bottom, then gradually raise it nearly to the surface, and so continue to troll till you feel a bite, which you will distingnish by perceiving a sudden catch or tug at your bait: keep the line free, that nothing may impede the Jack or Pike in running away with the bait to his haunt; let him remain quiet about ten minutes to pouch the bait, then wind up the slack line, and strike. If there be any very strong weeds, piles, or any thing else which may endanger your tackle near the place where you have hooked the fish, keep him from running to such places, by weighing him out as soon as possible.

The tackle used for trolling being very strong, I do not lose much time in playing these fish, at least in no comparison with what is necessary in killing Carp or Barbel: if you feel a bite, and the Jack or Pike soon stops, then runs again, and continues so to act, you may expect he is more on the play than the feed, therefore there is little chance of his pouching your bait; in this case it is advisable to strike, and you may be fortunate enough to hook the fish by some part, and secure him.

In fishing with a live bait, I prefer a Gudgeon to any other bait, besause it is a very strong fish, and lives longest on the hook; it is certainly a favorite with Jack, Pike, Perch and Chub: when so fishing, put a barrel shaped cork float (not very large) on your line, and a few swan shot to sink it three parts under water; cast your bait in search in the same way as directed with the gorge hook, adjust the float so that the bait may swim something below mid-water, and let it continue to swim about some minutes without taking it out, unless it comes too near shore, or hangs in the weeds. When the Jack or Pike takes this live bait, it is with much violence, and the float disappears instantly; therefore be sure always to keep your winch unlocked and line free (a good angler never fishes with the winch locked): give him ten minutes to pouch, and then strike.

In fishing with a live bait, the Jack and Pike will frequently take the bait, and sail about, holding it across their mouths by the middle, but will not pouch it, I then put on a spring snap hook, and strike the moment my float disappears. I have some acquaintances who never angle for Jack, Pike or Perch, any other way than with a small spring snap hook, the upper hook lodged beside the back fin of a live bait, and a small barrel shaped cork float to their line, and they kill many heavy fish. When you fish with a snap hook, (either the spring or plain,) you cast in search exactly as with the gorge; but when you feel a bite, strike quickly and hard, that your hooks may get firm hold of the Jack or Pike.

In the summer, when the rivers and other waters are much choaked with weeds, you may sometimes find a Jack in an opening, they then lie dozing near the surface: drop a baited snap hook in such place, and let it sink a few inches, and it is very probable he will take it; in this case your line should be very strong as well as the rod, for you must strike and lift the fish out instantly, or you lose both Jack and hook among the weeds.

In trolling with the bead hook, cast in the bait, as before directed with the gorge, &c. the lead in its mouth will cause it to sink gradually, but will not prevent its swimming about for some time: when at the bottom, you must raise it near to the surface again, and occasionally take it out and cast in a fresh place, either to the right, left, or opposite, taking care to fish every yard of water where the place is likely to yield a Jack or Pike; for it sometimes happens they are not much inclined to move, but will readily take a bait if it swims within their reach. When you feel a bite, let him run, and allow him ten minutes time for pouching before you strike.

Various other ways are practised for taking Jack, Pike and Perch, by night-lines, trimmers, &c.; but such methods are justly reprobated by the true angler, who exercises his skill and art for amusement more than profit. By those night lines and trimmers, many of the largest Pike and Perch are killed, The trimmers most used in pools, ponds, and still waters, are thrown in baited, and frequently left all night, and are taken up from a boat: if the place is not too broad, you may get them with your drag. These trimmers are made of strong thin cord, with a hook tied to gymp and wound on a piece of flat cork about five inches in diameter, with a groove to admit the line; the hook is baited with a Gudgeon, Roach, or some small fish: you then draw as much line out as admits the bait to hang about a foot from the bottom. There is a small slit in the cork, that you pass the line in, to prevent it unwinding; as soon as the Pike or Jack seizes the bait, the line loosens, and runs from the groove of the cork free, and allows the fish to retire to his haunt, and pouch at leisure.

These trimmers are named by many, the *man-of-war* trimmers.

The bank runner is mostly used in the day, while the angler is fishing for Roach, Barbel, &c. These trimmers are stuck in the bank, having strong turned wood sharpened for the purpose, with a winder at top for the line, which is fitted in the same manner as the man-of-war, but you must have a small cork float, and bait with live fish, which should swim about a foot from the ground. These kind of trimmers and night-lines are kept ready fitted at the fishing-tackle shops.

The season for trolling commences in July, and continues to the end of February, when the sportsman discontinues taking Jack, Pike and Perch, they being then full of spawn. These fish will certainly take a bait very free in March and April, and are in good condition for the table, but the angler is not allowed to troll for them in any of the subscription waters.

The most likely places to find Jack and Pike are near the end of scowers, and in deep eddies, in tumbling-bays, and where there is a bend and deep still water in a river, and near beds of land-dock weeds; also at the mouths of ditches or streams that empty themselves into rivers or ponds, and near flood-gates, and bull-rushes in lakes, canals, &c. during floods and while the water is thick in rivers, Jack get into the ditches and small streams or pieces of water that communicate with the river, but lay out of the current, and by which means are often tolerably clear, while the main river is thick, then troll in these places.

Trolling has some advantages over other modes of angling, for when the weather is boisterous and cold, you may take Jack and Pike, while other fish refuse every enticement; it is also highly conducive to health by the exercise which it affords; when the water is somewhat thick troll close in shore, for at such times Jack as well as other fish are found near the sides in rivers or other waters.

The Jack, Pike, and Perch generally bite most free during a breeze of wind, and will feed all day. When you intend to use live baits, take at least six in your fish kettle, and give them fresh water during your perambulation; if you mean to use the gorge, bait three hooks before you begin, and keep them in bran, in a gentle box large enough for the baits to lie at their length. Always use fresh and lively baits, for though Jack and Pike are tyrants and gluttons, they are also epicures.

C

CHAP. IV.

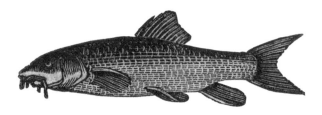

BARBEL.

——————— With hurried steps
The anxious angler paces on, nor looks aside,
Lest some brother of the angle, ere he arrives,
Possess his favourite swim.

THE Barbel only breed and thrive in rivers. In
the Thames and part of the river Lea there are
many, very fine and large: they are a handsome
fish, but their flesh is coarse, and therefore considered but of little value for the table; yet I have
been told they eat very well when baked, with
veal stuffing in their belly, as do the smaller size
split and fried. The Barbel is prized for being a
game fish, affording excellent sport to the angler,
mixed with some labour and anxiety. When of a
large size, they are exceeding crafty, sulky, and
strong, struggling a long time after they are
hooked, often lying motionless at the bottom many
minutes, then running under banks, or into large
beds of weeds, in fact, trying every possible way
to get off the hook, or break your line, which they
certainly will effect if you are deficient in skill, or

your tackle is in any way faulty. They are generally angled for on the river Thames in boats, called *punts,* with a stout rod, running tackle, gut line, cork float, and No. 6 or 7 hook; likewise with the ledger line, which is fitted in the following manner: a short solid rod, running tackle without a float, with hook No. 4 or 5 tied on twisted gut, baited with two marsh worms, or greaves. About ten inches above the hook is placed a piece of flat lead, perforated, (sold at the shops) below which is fixed a large shot to prevent the lead slipping down: the bait is then cast in, and lies clear on the ground; hold the top of your rod over the side of the boat, nearly touching the water, you will feel a bite, and at the second tug strike hard.

In the river Lea, you fish with much finer tackle: your rod either of bamboo or cane, with a stiff top, running tackle, fine gut line, quill float, and No. 8 or 9 hook; baits, red worms, gentles, and greaves. (Note, the bait must always touch the ground.) Greaves are certainly the most killing bait; but when I fish for Barbel, I always take the three baits with me, alternately putting worms. To bait your hook with a worm use the following method: enter the point of the hook in the worm a little below its head, and carry it down within a quarter of an inch of its tail, which part by its moving about entices the fish to bite; keep the shank of the hook as much covered with the body of the worm as you can; if yout put two worms on the hook draw the first up above the shank to the line while you put the second on; then draw the first down close on the second, the hook and shank is then well covered, and gentles, or greaves and a worm, on the hook together, as they sometimes want much enticement.—If the current is rapid let your bait drag two or three inches on the ground when fishing for Barbel or Chub either morning, noon, or night.

The Barbel bites very sharp and sudden, you must strike the instant and smartly, immediately raise the top of your rod, let him run some considerable distance before you attempt to turn him, then endeavour to keep your fish away from the shelves and beds of weeds, take him from the current into deep and still water as soon as possible and play him till he has quite lost his strength before you attempt to land him.

Before you begin to angle for Barble, throw in plenty of ground bait (you can hardly give them too much), and continue to do so frequently while fishing for them; the best ground bait is made with soaked greaves and clay, mixed together, in balls the size of an egg, also clay and gentles: indent a piece of clay, in which put some gentles, close it lightly, and the gentles will work out gradually, when at the bottom of the river.—Use this ground bait only in still holes. A quantity of worms, if they can be procured, chopped into small pieces, are likewise a good ground bait.

The Barbel feed from May till October, all the day, but best in the morning and evening: indeed, the chance of success increases with the coming night. They will even bite all night, and will feed very freely after rain, when the water is thickened a little.

REMARKS ON BARBEL.

The Barbel spawn in April: they delight to lie in deeps, in eddies, at the end of scowers, and under beds of weeds, and banks, routing up the gravel or sand with their noses, like pigs. The largest Barbel in the river Lea are taken in the Horse and Groom subscription water at Lea-bridge, some weighing upwards of fourteen pounds: a friend of mine (Mr. R.) took one here on Saturday, the 21st of May, 1814, which weighed twelve pounds. There are likewise fine Barbel as far up this river as Waltham-abbey, particularly at Tottenham-mills, in Bannister's water, Mr. Bowerbank's, (the last is private property) and in the subscription water at Bleak-hall, Edmonton—Barbel are very rarely taken as high up as Broxbourn and Hoddesden. The heaviest Barbel in the river Thames are taken at Chertsey-bridge, Shepperton, Walton, and Hampton-deeps. Barbel are also taken at Thames Ditton, Kingston, Twickenham, and Richmond.

CHAP. V.

CHUB.

THE Chub is a river fish, rather bony, and not very choice food, particularly in summer; they are firmer and better tasted during the winter months. The Chub will feed all the year, and is a bold-biting fish either at the top of the water or bottom, greedily taking flies, cockchafers, bees, &c. of which I shall speak when treating on fly-fishing.

When angling for Chub, where you have reason to expect a heavy fish, use running tackle, gut line, quill float, and hook No. 8 or 9. Strike the moment you perceive a bite, and let run, for the Chub, when struck, generally run furiously to the middle or opposite side before stopping; therefore it is necessary to give plenty of line, otherwise your fish will break away in the first instance. He is not so game a fish as the Barbel, for after his first effort, and a few plunges, you may venture to look at him, and soon after bring him to the shore or landing net. The baits for Chub are greaves; (to bait a hook with greaves use the following method: select the whitest pieces, and put four or five on your hook, or enough to cover it from the bend over the point, those pieces should be about half the size of a sixpence, and put on the hook one piece after the other;) red worms, gentles, paste, and bullock's brains, or pith from the back bone. Trolling or angling with a live Minnow is often successfully practised, particularly in spring, by which method many large Chub are taken. At this season, red worms are also good bait; put two on your hook, for the Chub loves a large bait: in the summer months, gentles and greaves; during winter, bullock's brains or pith is a killing bait; when that bait is not to be procured, use paste made of bread and honey. Before you begin to angle for Chub, throw in plenty of ground bait, and frequently while you are fishing, of the same sort as used for Barbel, or made with soaked bread, pollard, and bran, worked together: they bite during the whole day, but best in the morning and evening, in summer until quite dark, and all night. Fish as near the middle of the stream as you can in the spring months, and let the bait drag two or three inches on the ground.

REMARKS ON CHUB.

Chub never thrive in ponds or canals, but delight in deep holes, scowers, tumbling bays, &c. in rivers: in the autumn and cold weather they keep close in deep dark holes, or in the shelves under banks, and in holes that are shaded by large willow trees, whose branches hang close to or in the water. The river Lea is famous for large Chub from Temple-mills, or Lea-bridge, all the way to Hoddesden and Ware. The Chub will feed all the year.

> Both Chub and Roach will bite the whole year round,
> The bait should touch and lightly drag the ground.

CHAP. VI.

ROACH.

Hope and Patience support the fisherman.

THE rivers Thames and Lea breed an amazing number of Roach: although they are not considered a very delicious fish, I by no means think them indifferent food when in season, particularly if they are of a tolerable size, and caught in a river. By some persons they are considered a silly fish, and easily to be taken; but it requires much skill and practice, and a quick and steady eye, before any can pretend to the character of a good Roach angler.

Angling for Roach in the Thames is generally practised in boats, with fine gut line, and No. 10 hook; but I have killed many heavy Roach from its banks with a cane rod, quill float, single hair line, and No. 12 hook, in the holes and eddies between Chertsey-bridge and Shepperton, and from thence, by Haliford, Walton, and Sunbury, to Hampton, in the course of which rout the angler will find many good holes and swims: also in the meadows at Teddington, and on the opposite side from Kingston to Richmond. To take Roach like an artist, you must use a light cane rod, near twenty feet long, with a fine light stiff top, a single hair line, a tip-cap'd float, and No. 12 hook: observe when fishing, your line above the float must not be more than twelve or fourteen inches long, or you will not hit a fine bite; the float should be so shotted that not much more than an eighth of an inch appear above the water, for Roach (and very often the heaviest) bite so fine or gently, that without attending to the above nicety in adjusting your line, you will loose the chance of two bites out of three. Always keep the top of your rod over the float, and when you see the least movement of it, strike quickly, but lightly, (the motion coming from your wrist, not from the arm) or you break the line; if you have hit or hooked a fish, raise the top of your rod, keeping him as much under the top as you can, the butt down nearly touching the ground, and by playing him carefully he will soon be your own; in this fine fishing it is best to take with you a landing net, particularly if you fish off a high bank, or you hazard breaking in weighing the fish out.

The best bait for Roach is paste, made of second-day's-baked white bread, slightly dipped in water, which must be immediately squeezed out again, then place it in the palm of your left hand, and knead it with the thumb and finger of your right, until of a proper consistence: Roach will take this paste nearly the whole year, and by adding a little vermillion, it will be of a pink colour, which they sometimes prefer; in summer they will also take gentles, and in the spring and autumn sometimes blood and red worms, but paste is the most killing bait: put a piece on the hook about the size of a pea. Before you begin, plumb the depth accurately, and let your bait gently touch the bottom; you should occasionally take the depth again, particularly if the fish leave off feeding. Ground-bait plentifully before you begin with small balls of the same mixture as used for Chub and Barbel fishing, and, while angling, cast some in frequently (or chewed bread) close to the float.

REMARKS ON ROACH.

Roach breed and thrive in canals, ponds, and rivers: in rivers they are found on the shallows, in eddies, and in deep holes, also about bridges, piles, and locks; in ponds, near flood-gates, and those parts where the bottom is sandy. They bite all the year in rivers, but only during the summer months in ponds. Very large Roach are sometimes taken under Lea-bridge.

CHAP. VII.

DACE.

THE Dace is a very handsome fish, and considered as light nutritious food: they also afford the angler much sport, generally biting bold. They are angled for with the same sort of tackle as is used in Roach fishing: indeed, where you find Roach in rivers, you will frequently take Dace; but they are more likely to take your bait when angling for Barbel, with greaves or red worms, than the Roach, and will also rise more at a fly.

When you angle in a place more likely for Dace than Roach, which happens in the spring, on scowers, you may use a hook one size larger than for Roach, particularly if you bait with a red worm, which they are fond of at this season; in summer, put two gentles on your hook, or a small piece of greaves and a gentle on the point: greaves is the best bait for large Dace.

REMARKS ON DACE.

The Dace is a river fish, and will not thrive in ponds, or still waters. They do not bite much later in the season than October, but you may begin to fish for them in March.—Ground-bait the same as for Roach, or with only bran and clay mixed, and thrown into the water frequently.

CHAP. VIII.

GUDGEON.

THE Gudgeon is a sweet and mild fish, and much prized at the table when large and fresh caught: the rivers Thames and Lea boast of very fine and immense numbers. They are a bold biting fish, and afford much amusement to the young angler: they may be taken from April till October, all the day. In the Thames they are generally fished for with a red worm, gut or hair line, light cork float, and No. 10 hook. They spawn three times in the year, and are best for the table in the spring.

In the river Lea they angle with much finer tackle for Gudgeon, and bait with blood worms, using a light rod, single hair line, quill float, and No. 12 hook: the same tackle is also used in the New River.

REMARKS ON GUDGEONS.

Angling for Gudgeons commences in April in the river Lea: the best place in this river is in the subscription-water at the Horse and Groom, near Lea-bridge, where many dozens are taken daily until July, when they move to deeper water, and are caught occasionally while fishing for Roach, &c. Gudgeons are taken on the shallows, where the river is free from weeds, and the bottom is gravel or sand, which must be frequently stirred while fishing, with a long rake made for the purpose; in this way of angling you often hook a small Perch, and sometimes a Salmon Trout: plumb the depth before you begin, and let the bait touch the ground.

The New River, and the canals near London, have Gudgeons, but they are not so large as those caught in the Thames and Lea; in which rivers I have frequently taken thirty dozen in the course of a day's angling.

CHAP. IX.

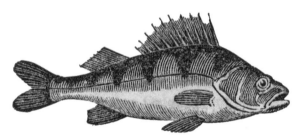

PERCH.

The bright-eyed Perch with fins of Tyrian dye.

THE Perch is reckoned a firm nutritious fish, excelled by none of the fresh water tribe: they are a bold fish, and generally take a bait immediately it is offered. Strong tackle is used in angling for them, a cork float, gut line, or a twisted hair, and No. 8 hook: the usual bait for Perch is a worm, well scowered, either marsh brandling, or the red; I prefer putting two red worms on a hook instead of one of the other kind, which are larger. They are also angled for with a live Minnow, hooked by the lips or back fin: when fishing in this manner for Perch, you should always have running tackle on, for sometimes a Pike, Trout, or Chub will take it, and larger Perch are caught this way than with a worm; it is likewise necessary to give them a few minutes time to pouch, and, as they often run a considerable distance before they do this, without running tackle you certainly would break, or lose your fish. When you have a bite with a worm bait, let him run about the length of a yard, and then strike smartly: the bait should be about a foot from the bottom.—Some angle for Perch with two hooks on a line, one at mid-water, the other lower.

REMARKS ON PERCH.

Angling for Perch commences in February, and continues till October; but during the hot months Perch feed very little. Dark windy weather, if not too cold, is best for Perch fishing: they delight to lie about bridges, mill-pools, and near locks in navigable rivers and canals, in deep and dark still holes and eddies, in ponds about flood-gates, on the gravel or sandy parts, and near the sides of rushes. You need not wait long in a place, for if there are any Perch about, and are inclined to feed, they will soon take the bait. Shrimps boiled or unboiled are a good bait for Perch, especially in Docks, Canals, and tide; so are grubs; a large tough grey maggot found in light earth and among the roots of potatoes and turnips.

CHAP. X.

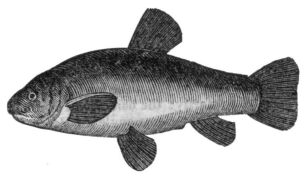

TENCH.

THE Tench is generally prized as a fine rich fish, but they are very scarce in most of the rivers and streams about London; some few are taken in the spring and summer out of the rivers Thames and Lea, also in the Camberwell and Croydon canals: I have caught very fine Tench in the river Roding, near the bridge called Red-bridge, at Wanstead, and several in the ponds in Wanstead-park. They take red worms in the spring, and gentles or sweet paste in the hot months: use a fine gut line, quill float, and No. 10 hook.

REMARKS ON TENCH.

The Tench will breed in rivers, lakes, and ponds, but they thrive best in ponds where the bottom is composed of loam, clay or mud; they bite very free in summer during warm, muggy, dark weather, and particularly while small fine rain descends in the evening or morning. Your bait should nearly touch the ground in ponds, but must drag in rivers: fish early and late.

CHAP. XI.

CARP.

The yellow Carp, with scales bedropp'd with gold.

THE Carp is a beautiful fish, and much prized by many for its richness, particularly when stewed in wine. They are not very numerous either in the river Thames or Lea, what are caught are remarkable fine and large. The Carp is very shy in biting at a bait, particularly the large ones, who seem to increase in cunning and craft with their weight: in angling for them, use running tackle, a small quill float, fine clear gut line, and No. 9 hook; indeed, you must fish as fine as the nature of the water will allow, or you have little chance of

D

taking Carp. They will begin to feed in rivers the latter end of February if the weather is mild, from which time till the end of April they generally bite more free than at any other part of the season, which goes out with October. The best bait (particularly at the first of the season) is well scowered red worms; in the summer, gentles and paste: I frequently bait my hook with a red worm, and a gentle at the point, and with much success. Paste made with honey, as follows, will be found a killing bait for Carp towards the autumn: take the crumb of new-baked bread, dip it in honey, and work it well together—you may use a piece nearly as large as a marble for a bait; when fishing with this bait in still water, the Carp will suck in the paste so sly, that without you keep a watchful eye, your bait will be gone without your discovering a bite. In fishing for Carp, keep as far from the water as you can, and, if convenient, you should ground-bait the place you intend angling in, the night before, and also plumb the depth, that you may not have occasion to disturb the water when you begin to angle. Those who are inclined, or have an opportunity to pursue this plan, will find they have not lost their labour. Carp will seldom bite in the middle of the day, unless soft light rain descends: the best time is as soon as you can see your float in the water, and late in the evening. When you have hooked a Carp, give line, use him gently, and with patience, for they are very strong fish in the water, and will try every way to get off the hook. Ground-bait the same as for Roach, and when angling with sweet paste, frequently throw a few small pieces of it in close to your float: let your bait swim about an inch from the bottom when angling in still water, but it must touch the bottom when fishing in a river or stream.

REMARKS ON CARP.

Carp will thrive well in rivers, but they only breed in still waters, canals, lakes, ponds, &c. they are found in deep holes by or near flood-gates, in eddies, and near large beds of weeds. They will not feed in ponds later than Michaelmas, nor earlier than May, unless the weather is particularly mild.

***

CHAP. XII.

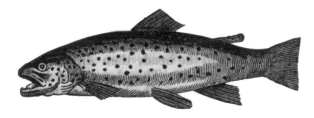

TROUT.

Swift Trout, diversified with crimson spots.

THE Trout is a very beautiful fish both in form and colour, and is excelled by none of the fresh-

water breed as a delicacy at table: they are vora-
cious, like the Pike, and destroy multitudes of
Minnows, and other small fish. The Trout often
affords the angler much sport, for they are an exceeding strong and game fish: in angling for them
at bottom, use a strong rod, running tackle, and
No. 6 hook; when you bait with worms, which is
the best method in the early part of the morning,
and late at night, also during the day, if the water
is much coloured, and the weather dull or boisterous, angle without a float, putting sufficient
shot on the line to sink the bait—the shot to be
placed about eight or nine inches above the hook.
This bait must be one large lob worm, or two marsh
or dew worms, well scowered, and very lively;
put the two worms on the hook in the following
manner: run the point of your hook in at the top
of the first worm's head, and bring it out about
three parts down the body, then draw it carefully
up over the arming or whipping of the hook, while
you put on the other; enter the point of your hook
in the second worm something below the middle,
and carry it near to the head, then draw the first
worm round to join it. This done, cast in your
bait, and let it gently drag the bottom: when a fish
begins to bite, do not strike the first time you feel a
tug, but rather slacken your line; when you feel
two or three sharp tugs, then strike smartly, and
if a heavy fish, give him line, and be not in too
great haste to land him.

—— With yielding hand feeling him still,
Yet to his furious course give way,
Till floating broad upon his breathless side,
You safely drag your spangled prize on shore.

The Trout is very strong, and struggles most violently; sometimes, as soon as he feels the hook, he will leap out of the water more than a foot high, and on falling again, will fly about in every direction, to the great alarm of the angler for his rod, line or hook.

And flies aloft, and flounces round the pool.

I have taken many Trout when the water has been too bright for using strong tackle, by putting two or three yards of fine gut at the bottom, with a No. 10 hook, baited with one red worm of the largest size, well scowered. Run the point of the hook in near the tail, and draw the worm over the whipping or arming of your hook, the point and barb will then lie near the head; in this state, cast in the stream opposite you, and let it sink gradually, and swim down some yards below, then draw it up nearly to the surface, let it sink again, and so continue till you bring it near you. If a bite, act as directed with the strong running tackle, to which this two or three yards of fine must be fastened.

The Minnow is a most killing bait for a Trout, particularly when used by spinning it against the stream, or in the eddies, where the water falls over into tumbling-bays, mill-tails, pools, &c. Hooks are fitted on purpose for this mode of angling by the tackle-makers. When you are thus fishing, use strong tackle, and cast your bait lightly in the water, and draw against the stream or eddy very near the surface, so that you can see the Minnow: if you are angling from a high bridge, or any eminence, it will be best to let your bait be some considerable distance from you, particularly if the water is bright; this way of angling for Trout is often very successful, and the largest fish are taken by it. When a bite, let him run a little before you strike: in fishing with a live Minnow, hook it by the lips, or beneath the back fin; put on a small cork float, No. 6 hook, and let your bait swim below mid-water. Deep dark holes, that are free from eddies or stream, are the most likely to take a Trout in, when fishing with a live Minnow. Trout are also taken with flies, both natural and artificial, which I shall describe under the head of fly-fishing.

REMARKS ON TROUT.

Trout will begin to feed in March, if the weather is fine for the season, and continue till Michaelmas: about a month after this time they spawn. The first two or three months are the best for bottom-fishing; the Trout are then on the scowers and shallows, and feed most at bottom, the weather being frequently cold and unsettled, so that few flies are found on the water till the middle of May. In the summer season especially, the large Trout love to lie in deep holes and eddies, near mill-tails and pools; sometimes close to the apron, which is a good place to drop in a worm bait. You cannot be too early or late in fishing for Trout, as they seldom feed in the day, unless after a flood, or in dark weather, accompanied with a good breeze of wind.

The London angler has seldom the pleasure of bringing home a dish of Trout caught in either the river Thames or Lea, for those rivers, however famous they may have been, at present contain but few: there are certainly many good Trust streams within twenty miles of the metropolis, but they are all private property. The river Wandle, particularly at Carshalton in Surrey, has numerous fine Trout; and again at Merton-mills, &c. till you arrive at Wandsworth. The little river called Ravensbourn, running from or by Sydenham, Lewisham, &c. to the Kent-road Greenwich, has Trout; also the Darent, or Dartford-creek, may boast of many very fine Trout at Crayford, Bexley, Foot's-Cray, Paul's-Cray, &c. and near the powder-mills, through and near Darent, and Horton, to Farningham in Kent. At Rickmansworth in Hertfordshire, and its neighbourhood, are several good Trout streams, and from thence to Uxbridge in Middlesex: at the latter place the angler may indulge himself in angling for Trout by paying a certain sum, but if he meets with any success he must also pay for the fish he takes.

CHAP. XIII.

CRUCIAN OR PRUSSIAN CARP.

T<small>HIS</small> fish is not very common in England. By some persons it is supposed to be a cross breed, between the Carp and Roach, as it favours both in appearance, the scales and head resembling the Carp, the fins and flat body the Roach; it is a poor bony fish, the flesh soft and insipid: the Crucian Carp seldom reach a pound weight. They breed frequently, for which reason they are useful in ponds, as food for the Jack and Pike, and large Eels are also fond of them; you may bait trimmers, night-lines and hooks, with the Crucians, to lay in ponds, moats, pits or canals with success, but I never found them good bait in a river. These fish breed, and are very numerous, in many ponds round London, particularly in those on Clapham common; they begin to feed in April, and continue until Michaelmas. You may take them either with a red worm, gentle, or paste. being a hungry bold biting fish, and will take a bait at any time of the day; use a gut or horse hair line, with a No. 11 or 12 hook, and fish at bottom: chewed bread is good ground bait for Crucian or Prussian Carp.

CHAP. XIV.

LOACH, OR STONE LOACH.

THIS is a very small fish without scales, has a round body, with whattels or barbs at its mouth, like the Barbel; it seldom exceeds four inches in length, and in colour it resembles the Tench, or the golden hue of the Minnow. I havs heard they are a delicious fish when fried in batter, or with egg and bread; but there is some difficulty in catching a dish of them, being scarce as well as small. The Stone Loach is an excellent, indeed, a most killing bait for large Eels, used on night lines; they are generally to be found in small gravelly brooks and rivulets—I have sometimes taken a few in the river Lea, in the shallows, near mill tails: they lie at the bottom, routing the gravel the same as Barbel. You may take them with the tail end of a red worm, and a small hook, during the warm weather.

THE PRICKLEBACK, OR STICKLEBACK,

is the smallest of the finny tribe; they are some-times used as a bait in fishing for Perch: in this case you must cut off the prickly fin on their back. They are caught in all the ditches and ponds round London, with a small piece of worm.

CHAP. XV.

BLEAK AND MINNOW.

BLEAK are found in the rivers Thames, Lea, and the New River, in immense numbers; they are handsome fish, but do not grow to a large size, seldom exceeding two ounces in weight, and not much valued for their flavour: they are a lively sportive fish, and easily taken with a small fly at the top of the water, and with paste or gentles at mid-water, or at the bottom. Angle for them with a light rod, single hair line, small quill float, and No. 12 or 13 hook. They will bite all day from April till October, affording the young angler sport and practice: these may be caught in all parts of the New River, from Sadler's Wells to Ware. I have found the greatest sport in angling for Bleak to bait with one gentle on a No. 12 or 13 hook, and fish about a foot deep, using a hair line, very small quill float, and keep continually throwing in half a dozen gentles for ground-bait, or a little chewed bread.

MINNOW.

Minnows are also very numerous in the Thames, Lea, and New River. They are a very small fish, and little valued by the angler excepting for baits, when fishing for Trout, Perch, or Chub; the Minnow bites very freely at a blood worm, a small piece of red worm, gentles, or paste—the tackle should be very light, and a No. 13 hook: they are taken all day from March till winter.

———

CHAP. XVI.

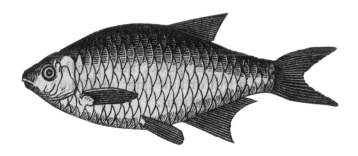

BREAM, RUDD, POPE, AND MILLER'S THUMB.

The Bream is a very bony fish, and of little worth; they are not very numerous either in the river Thames or Lea, but abound in Weybridge, Byfleet, and the Mole rivers, and in Dagenham-breach. They are more frequently taken in the spring than at any other time, when angling for Carp with a red worm.

RUDD.

THE Rudd is a very indifferent fish for the table; in shape and colour it is much like the Roach, and tinged with gold. They thrive best in ponds, but seldom exceed a pound in weight; they will take red worms, paste, and gentles, during summer: use a gut or hair line, quill float, No. 11 hook, and angle at bottom.

POPE OR RUFF.

THE Pope or Ruff is much like the Perch in form and flavour, being firm and well-tasted; they are taken with worms and gentles, but are rarely to be met with in the vicinity of London.

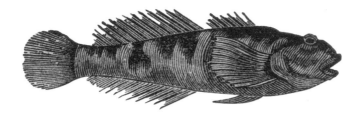

.MILLER'S THUMB.

THE Miller's Thumb is a small ugly fish, hardly worth naming: in warm weather they lie in the shallow waters, on stones, and will take a small piece of worm directly you put it near them. These fish are only found in rivers.

CHAP. XVII.

EELS.

EELS are found in all rivers, canals, and ponds near London in great numbers, and remarkably fine: they are taken with the rod and line, and with night line, dead lines, and bobbing.

Gut or twisted hair lines with a float, and No. 9 or 10 hook, should be used when fishing with a rod; bait with a worm, and fish at the bottom.

The most convenient way of fishing with the dead line, is to use the bank runner, with a whipcord line, on which you may put five or six hooks, about nine inches apart. The night line is much stronger, and should be baited with small fish, or lob worms.

Bobbing for Eels is practised in a boat, with a large bunch of worms suspended by a strong cord from a pole or stout rod, in the following manner: first of all, you must procure a large quantity of worms, (marsh worms are best,) and string them on worsted, by passing a needle through them from head to tail, until you have as many strung as will form a bunch as large as a good-sized turnip, then fasten them on the line so that all the ends may hang level. In the middle is placed a piece of lead, of a conical form, which may be got at any of the fishing-tackle shops, made for the purpose; thus prepared, cast the baits into the water gently, let them sink to the bottom, and then keep raising them a few inches from the ground, and dropping them again, until you have a bite, which is easily perceived, as the Eel tugs very strongly : be as expert as possible, and at the same time as steady in raising your line, so that your fish in dropping off, may fall into the boat. Immense numbers are taken by this method. During the hot weather, fish in rather shoal water, and out of the stream.

SNIGGLING FOR EELS.

By sniggling, many good Eels are taken in the river Lea, and various streams about the metropolis, during the summer months, when the waters are low. A line for sniggling may be made of a few yards of strong plaited silk, such as is used in trolling for Pike, or common whipcord; instead of a hook use a stout worsted needle, to the middle of which tie the line, and bait with a small lob, or large marsh worm, very tough, and well scowered: enter the point of the needle at the top or head of your worm, and draw it up over the needle and line, so as completely to cover it. You carry the line in your hand on a winder, searching for Eels between the planks of the aprons of mill-tails, flood-gates, wharfings, piles, and bridges; also in holes in the banks of rivers, canals, and ponds, and in sandy muddy ditches, where you will frequently find them lying with their heads nearly out of their hiding-places, waiting for the chance of food: use a stick, with a forked top to place the bait in the hole, when you will presently perceive a bite by the Eel's drawing the line further into his haunt: give him a minute or so to gorge, then strike smartly, which will immediately cause the needle to fall athwart in the fish's throat or stomach; hold the line tight, and he will soon make his appearance. The nearest place to London in the river Lea, where much success is to be met with by this mode of fishing, is at Lower Clapton: between this place and Tottenham-mills, on the east side near the Oil-mills, the angler will find several holes which contain good Eels, not only in the banks of the river, but in the ditches, and among the osiers and willows.

CHAP. XVIII.

FLOUNDER AND SMELT.

THE Flounder is only found in rivers where the tide flows: they are generally considered a very sweet fish, light and easy of digestion. In the creeks from Blackwall to Bromley, Stratford, and West-Ham, they are taken either with dead lines or floated, in the same manner as Eels; in fact, when you angle for Eels in this part you angle for Flounders, as they will both take the same baits at the same season, and it frequently happens that you take both Flounders and Eels promiscuously. See fishing for Eels with a floated line.

SMELTS

are well known as most delicious fish: they are caught by angling, in the following manner: you must have an exceeding stiff and strong top to your rod, a strong gut line, heavy float, and from ten to twelve hooks, about eight or nine inches apart, the hooks will stand better from the line if tied on a fine bristle.—Use No. 9 hooks, baited with a small piece of an Eel, or pieces of a smelt, the bottom hook touching the ground.—Note, when they bite they throw the float up, all other fish pull it down.

They are sometimes fished for without a float, having a small piece of lead at bottom, which you let touch the ground, gently raising and sinking it till you feel a bite: this is called dip fishing, from the name of the lead (which may be procured at the tackle shops), and is the most destructive way of killing Smelts. The best place to catch these fish near London, is in the canal that runs from Limehouse-hole to Blackwall, through the Isle of Dogs; they are also frequently taken off the logs lying in the Thames, and in all the Wet Docks, below London bridge. You may fish for Smelts from July to November and December; very early and late is the most successful time: many will take twenty dozen in a day.

DEAD LINES.

A great many Eels, Flounders, &c. are taken with dead lines, between Blackwall and Old-Ford, in the several creeks round Bromley, West-Ham, Abbey-Mills and Stratford, where the tide flows from the river Thames. The dead line is made of whipcord, generally about six yards in length, to which is affixed five or six hooks, which should be tied on pieces of bristle, twisted hair or gut, not more than four inches long, with a loop at the end: No. 9 is the hook generally chosen for this purpose. Loop the hooks on the line (beginning at the bottom) about a foot apart; close to every hook put a large shot, or piece of lead, to keep the bait on the ground, as every hook must lie at the bottom, for which purpose you should throw sufficient length of

E

line into the water. Flounders and Eels seldom take a bait unless it lies on the ground: the best bait is a red worm; indeed, no other bait than worms is likely to succeed. Fishing in this way, you may use half a dozen lines at a time, by casting them in a few yards from each other, and tying the line to a weed or a small stick, stuck in the ground or bank. It is necessary to have a short rod with you, three or four yards long, to the top of which is fixed a small iron crutch or fork; with this rod you take up the lines in the following manner: take the line in your left hand, and with the right pass the crutch or fork under the line, pushing it forward in the water some distance, by which means you can easily lift out your line over weeds, or any other impediment. Without this rod or crutch, you would be compelled to drag the lines up the side or bank, where the hooks would catch and spoil the baits, and occasion you infinite trouble. It is astonishing how great a number of Flounders, Eels, Perch, Dace, Roach and Gudgeons, are caught by this method of fishing in those creeks I have named, particularly from an hour after high water till the tide is quite run out: you may begin to use dead lines in April, and meet sport until November.

CHAP. XIX.

ARTIFICIAL FLY FISHING.

FISHING with an artificial fly is certainly a very pleasant and gentlemanly way of angling, and is attended with much less labour and trouble than bottom fishing. The fly fisherman has but little to carry either in bulk or weight, nor has he the dirty work of digging clay, making ground-baits, &c. he may travel for miles with a book of flies in his pocket, and a light rod in his hand, and cast in his bait as he roves on the banks of a river, without soiling his fingers, it is therefore preferred by many to every other way of angling: yet fly fishing is not without its disadvantages, for there are many kinds of fish that will not take a fly, whereas, all the different species the fresh waters produce or breed, will take a bait at bottom at some season of the year; and it is also worthy of notice, that the angler who fishes at bottom, has many months and days in the year when the fish will so feed, consequently he has frequent opportunities of enjoying his amusement, when the fly fisherman is entirely deprived of the chance of sport by very cold or wet weather, the winter season, &c. Many good Jack and Pike are taken at Christmas, but at that season of the year neither Trout or Chub are likely to rise for a fly, however skilfully made or thrown. Fly fishing certainly partakes more of science than bottom fishing, and of course requires much time,

study, and practice, before the angler can become
any thing like an adept at making or casting a fly;
indeed, artificial fly fishing is difficult to learn, and
more difficult to describe. The young angler will
gain more information on the subject by attending
a fly fisherman a few months, while he is following
the amusement, than he can by perusing all the
works ever written on the subject; however, I will
endeavour to direct him in the choice of tackle,
flies, &c. in the most plain and concise manner
possible; also how to cast or throw his flies in
search, and where he is most likely to find fish.

I should recommend the young fly fisherman in
the first instance, to purchase his artificial flies, but
after some little experience in the art, by all means
to make his own. I would likewise strongly advise
him to court the friendship or acquaintance of an
experienced fly fisher, for without some practical
knowledge, he will never attain to much eminence
in the science.

CHAP. XX.

ARTIFICIAL FLIES.

THERE are upwards of a hundred different kind of flies made for fly fishing; a selection of which I shall describe, suitable for every month during the season: they may be purchased at a small expence. By using these flies, and practising the art of casting or throwing his fly, the young angler will sooner acquire the skill of killing fish by fly fishing, than by encumbering himself with a stock of dubbing, hair, wool, feathers, &c. for manufacturing artificial flies before he is master of the art of throwing one.

Some anglers fish with a fly in winter, but little sport is ever met with before April, or much later than Michaelmas, unless the weather is unusually mild.

A LIST OF PALMERS FOR FLY FISHING, BEGINNING WITH APRIL.

The cow-dung fly may be used from the first of this month, and is a killing fly to the end. The brown or dun drake, is a good fly in the middle of the day, particularly if the weather proves gloomy. The horse fly will also take fish during the whole of April, but best late in the evening.

MAY.

The stone fly may be used all this month with much success, but more particularly in the mornings. The yellow May fly is a killing fly in the evenings. The black caterpillar fly is a good fly this month, in small rivers and Trout streams; it kills best in those days that succeed very hot mornings. The fly called the camlet, may be used with success all day until the middle of June, for small fish, but the green drake is the most killing.

JUNE.

The lady fly is now a good fly, particularly when the water begins to brighten after a flood. The black gnat fly is a killing fly in an evening, especially if the weather has been warm and showery during the day. The blue gnat is only used when the water is very fine and low. The red spinner will kill best when the water is dark, and late in the evening, still prefer the green drake.

JULY.

The orange fly is an excellent bait, particularly if this month proves close, hot, and gloomy weather. The large red ant fly is a killing fly for some hours in the middle of the day. The badger fly is a good fly in the early part of this month, and in the coolest days, but the green drake is better.

AUGUST.

The small red and black ant flies are good killers for three or four hours in the afternoon, and sometimes till sun-set, if it is occasionally obscured. The hazel fly, by some called the button fly, is a valuable fly all this month. The small fly, called the light blue fly, is known to most fly fishers to be a killing bait from morning till afternoon, if the weather is at all favourable.

SEPTEMBER.

The willow fly is most to be depended on this month, and for the remainder of the season: any of those noticed for July or August may also be used occasionally. All the flies I have enumerated, are for killing Trout; but you may also take Chub and Dace with them, and perchance a Salmon. For making these flies, mohair, of various colours, is used; also seal's wool, bear's and camel's hair, sheep's wool, badger's hair, hog's down, camlets of all colours, the fur of hares, squirrels, and foxes, feathers from the neck of the game cock, called hackles; likewise feathers from the peacock, mallard, the domestic hen, &c. &c. All these materials may be purchased at the shops.

———

CHAP. XXI.

CASTING OR THROWING THE LINE AND BAIT.

IN casting or throwing the line and fly, while yet a novice, draw out the line from the winch in length something more than the rod; but when you can manage it well, you may throw twice this length of line, and deliver your fly to within an inch of the spot you desire; to do this, raise your arm, and forming nearly a circle round your head by waving the rod, cast the line from you before you return your arm from the head, then draw the fly lightly and gently towards the shore, have a quick and attentive eye to your bait, for if a fish rises at it, and you omit that moment striking, the fish is lost, for they immediately discover the fraud, and throw the bait from their mouth. Thus continue to cast in your line in search, and fish every yard of water likely to afford sport, and never despair of success; for sometimes it so happens, that after many fruitless hours spent without a fish ever rising at your fly, you will fill your bag or basket during the last hour.

The lighter your fly and line descends on the water the greater the chance of a bite, for thereon

depends much of the advantage the experienced
angler has over the novice, and which is only to be
acquired by practice and love for the art. Never
use more than one hook on your line at a time, till
you feel fully confident you can throw your line,
with one, to any given distance or place: when you
commence fishing any water, endeavour to keep
the wind at your back, as it enables you to stand
further out of the fish's sight, and you have the ad-
ditional advantage of fishing both sides of the
stream, if not very broad. When casting your fly
in a small stream, and the middle should be shallow, (there is always a rippling on the water in
that part,) cast your bait to the opposite side, and
slowly draw it to the rippling, let it float down some
distance, and if the fish like your fly they will certainly take it; or if you see a fish rise in any part
of the water you are fishing in, immediately throw
your bait just beyond it, draw the fly gently
over the spot where the fish rose, and, if done
quickly and neatly, you will generally secure the
fish.

CHAP. XXII.
NATURAL FLY FISHING.

NATURAL fly fishing is generally termed dib-
bing, or dapping, which is practised with a stout
rod, having a stiff top, running tackle, strong line,

and No. 6 hook, for Trout and Chub: in this mode
of fishing, it is absolutely necessary that you stand
behind a tree, bush, high weeds, or something to
hide your person, or the fish will not rise at your
fly or bait; when such a spot or blind can be met
with in a stream where there are fish, this is a killing way of angling, particularly late in the evening.
You must draw out as much line as will just reach
the surface of the water, with the top of your rod
a little raised, and keep the bait in motion upon the
surface by gently raising and lowering the top part
of the rod; when a fish takes your bait, after
a moment or two, strike smartly, and if not too
large to endanger breaking, lift him out immediately, for by playing them while dapping, you are
very likely to scare away the others by exposing
yourself to their sight.

FOR TROUT,

the green drake fly is a killing bait during the
months of May and June: the grey drake is also a
good fly in these months, but not equal to the green.
The stone and hawthorn fly are very excellent flies,
and are killing baits from the latter end of April till
Midsummer: these flies are with much difficulty
kept alive, even for a day or two, therefore artificial
ones are generally used.

FOR CHUB,

the best bait during May, June and July, I have
found to be, in the day time, the humble, or by

some called the bumble-bee, and late in the evening a large white moth, bred in willow trees, &c. They will also take the cockchafer, grasshopper, the fly called the father-longlegs, and all kinds of moths and bees, but they generally prefer the largest: these baits are easily procured by persons who reside in the country, and kept alive: I prefer the live bait, and seldom use any other.

FOR DACE AND BLEAK,

the best bait is the common house fly: you may put two on a No. 10 hook. These flies are kept in a bottle. Dace are caught of the largest size by dapping, concealing yourself as for Trout and Chub.— For Bleak, one common house fly on a No. 12 hook.

CHAP. XXIII.

1.

2.

1. Rod to place and take up trimmers and dead lines.
2. A trimmer baited with a live bait.

TRIMMER ANGLING, AND HOW TO BOB AND LAY
NIGHT LINES FOR EELS.

THE line for a trimmer should be from sixteen to
twenty yards in length, which may be bought at
the fishing-tackle shops: to this line must be
fastened a double hook tied to gimp; about a foot
from the hook place a wine bottle cork fast on the
line, about two feet above the cork fasten a bullet.
To bait your hook, (suppose with a Gudgeon) take
your baiting-needle and hook it to the loop end of
the gimp to which the hook is tied, then enter the
point of your needle under the skin of the Gudgeon
near the back, about an inch from the head, and
carry it carefully between the skin and the flesh to
within an inch of the tail, then draw out the needle
and gimp till the hooks come to the place where the
needle first entered, then fasten the loop end of the
gimp to the line, and all is complete as represented
in the cut. Chuse a place to lay your trimmer free
from weeds, &c. and cast it in in the following
manner: having provided yourself with a forked
stick, hold the line with your left hand, the
forked stick in the right; put the forked part under
the line between the bullet and the cork, you may
then place the bait in any part of the water you
like: the common method is to fasten the line to a
peg-stick, which is stuck firmly in the ground,
laying the spare line in a coil, but fastening your
line to a bank-runner is much the best plan, because it prevents the chance of your line being

tangled, which sometimes occurs in the common method, and the fish is then checked before he pouches the bait, and immediately leaves it.—Note, if the hook is baited carefully in the manner I have directed, with a lively Gudgeon, it will live many hours in the water.

The method of taking Eels by night lines is as follows: take about ten yards of small strong cord, (sold at the tackle-shops,) tie one end to a stick or peg, which you fix firmly in the ground: small dead Roach, Dace, or Gudgeons, are better baits for Eels laid at night, than either worms, frogs, or chicken's guts. When you bait with a fish, you must have a double hook, (which are sold at the tackle-shops,) tied to gimp, wire, &c. called Eel hooks: to bait these hooks, you act exactly as directed in baiting the gorge for trolling, (see page 8). After fastening the hook to the line, place a bullet on the line about a foot from the hook, which keeps the line and baited hook in the place you lay it. If a number of lines so baited are fastened to a stout cord about two feet apart, and cast in the water; it is called a chain line, and is generally tied to a brick at one end, which is thrown in, and the other end securely fastened to a tree or strong peg fixed in the bank. Eels are also taken chiefly during night and fishing from a boat) by bobbing with a large bunch of worms suspended by a strong cord from a pole; about a pint of worms should be strung on stout worsted or thin twine, then gather them up in a bunch; in the middle of them place a piece of lead of a conical shape, (sold at the tackle-shops;) place the broad end downwards, fasten the whole to the cord which is tied to the pole, let them sink to the bottom, raising and falling them a few inches until you feel the Eels bite, then raise up the worms steadily, and the Eels will drop off into the boat.

CHAP. XXIV.

RULES, OBSERVATIONS, AND LAWS RELATIVE TO ANGLING.

To prevent disputes, it is generally understood and agreed to among anglers, that a distance the length of rod and line, or thirty feet, shall be kept between each person while angling.

When you have made choice of a place to fish, first plumb the depth truly, and with as little disturbance to the water as may be; let your line with the plummet to it remain in the water while you make and cast in the ground bait, by which time the line will be softened and stretched, consequently less likely to break, if you should hook a fish soon after commencing: if the water is still, throw in small pieces of ground bait, and keep as far from the water as you can.

Accustom yourself to use fine tackle, which will the sooner make you a skilful angler by the care requisite in using such tackle: if you perchance break your tackle, do not lose your temper,* but sit down, and diligently repair the damage done, and begin again, recollecting that "Hope and "Patience support the fisherman."

When soft rain falls, or the day turns out foggy and close, most kind of fish will feed.

If hail falls, or the day proves very cold, and the wind blows strong, either from east, south, west, or north, the angler must not expect much sport:

> If ask'd, "What winds suit angling best?"
> I answer, "The south, or south-west."

For your health's sake never drink water out of rivers or ponds while in a perspiration: also be careful to keep your feet dry, by wearing strong boots or shoes.

> Whene'er dear brothers you shall go to fish,
> I wish you luck to take a handsome dish
> Of Carp, Tench, Pike, Perch, Barbel, Dace or Roach,
> By angling fair—I pray you never poach;
> But first, good sirs, a useful lesson take
> From an old brother *Bob,* an angling rake.
> Before you quit your homes, look round and think,
> If all your *traps* are right, with cash for meat and drink;
> Worms, gentles, paste and greaves you must provide,
> Good lines, floats, plummets, and spare hooks beside;
> And when your sport is done, bear this in mind—
> Look well about, that naught is left behind.

As an advocate for angling, I feel interested and anxious for the honour and credit of the angler's

---

* Good-nature sets our hearts at ease,
———and softens pain and sorrow.

character and conduct, therefore I beg his attention to a few observations and extracts from acts of parliament relative to the preservation of fish and fisheries. It should be recollected, that if the angler commits an offence or trespass from his ignorance of the laws on the subject, he is equally liable to fine and punishment as if acting by premeditated design; for it is presumed by the magistrates of courts, that from the known publicity of the laws, every person is acquainted with their regulations in respect to the protection of property, punishment for trespass, and the like. Moreover, as reasonable beings, and accountable for our misdeeds, it surely behoves us so to regulate our conduct in pursuing our pleasures and amusements, that we in no wise lose sight of or infringe the *Golden Rule,* that of "doing unto others as we would they should do unto us,"—a strict observance of which I seriously recommend to all brother anglers.

The most recent, and the principal act to protect fisheries, was passed in the fifth year of his present Majesty's reign, from which the following extract is taken:

"No one shall enter into any park or paddock fenced in and enclosed, or into any garden, orchard, or yard adjoining or belonging to any dwelling-house, in or through which park or paddock, garden, orchard or yard any river or stream of water shall run or be, or wherein shall be any river, pond, pool, moat, stew or other water; and by any ways, means or device whatsoever shall steal, take, kill or destroy any fish bred, kept or preserved in any such river or stream, pond, pool, moat, stew or other water aforesaid, without the consent of the owner or owners thereof, or shall be aiding or assisting in the stealing, taking, killing or destroying any such fish as aforesaid, or shall receive or buy any such fish, knowing the same to be stolen or taken as aforesaid, and being thereof indicted within six calendar months next after such offence or offences shall have been committed, before any judge or justices of gaol delivery for the county wherein such park or paddock, garden, orchard or yard shall be, and shall on such indictment be by verdict or by his or their own confession or confessions, convicted of any such offence or offences as aforesaid, the person or persons so convicted shall be transported for seven years.

"And for the more easy and speedy apprehending and convicting of such person or persons as shall be guilty of any of the offences before mentioned, be it further enacted by the authority aforesaid, that in case any person or persons shall at any time after the first day of June commit or be guilty of any such offence or offences as herein beforementioned, and shall surrender himself to any one of his Majesty's justices of the peace in and for the county where such offence or offences shall have been committed, or being apprehended and taken, or in custody for such offence or offences, or on any other account, and shall voluntarily make a full confession thereof, and a true discovery, upon oath of the person or persons who was or were his accomplice or accomplices in any of the said offences so as such accomplice or accomplices may be apprehended and taken, and shall on the trial of

F

such accomplice or accomplices give such evidence of such offence or offences as shall be sufficient to convict such accomplice or accomplices thereof, such person making such confession and discovery, and giving such evidence as aforesaid, shall, by virtue of this act, be pardoned, acquitted and discharged of and from the offence or offences so by him confessed as aforesaid.

"That in case any person or persons shall take, kill or destroy, or attempt to take, kill or destroy, any fish in any river or stream, pond, pool, or other water (not being in any park or paddock, or in any garden, orchard or yard adjoining or belonging to any dwelling-house, but shall be in any other inclosed ground which shall be private property) every such person being lawfully convicted thereof by the oath of one or more credible witness or witnesses, shall forfeit and pay for every such offence, the sum of five pounds to the owner or owners of the fishery of such river or stream of water, or of such pond, pool, moat or other water; and it shall or may be lawful to and for any one or more of his Majesty's justices of the peace of the county, division, riding or place where such last mentioned offence or offences shall be committed, upon complaint made to him or them upon oath against any person or persons for any such last mentioned offence or offences, to issue his or their warrant or warrants to bring the person or persons so complained of before him or them; and if the person or persons so complained of shall be convicted of any of the said offences last mentioned, before such justice or justices, or any other of his Majesty's justices of the same county, division, riding or place aforesaid, by the oath or oaths of one or more credible witnesses,

which oath such justice or justices are hereby authorised
to administer, or by his or their own confession, then and
in such case the party so convicted shall, immediately
after such conviction, pay the said penalty of five pounds,
hereby before imposed for the offence or offences aforesaid, to such justice or justices before whom he shall be
so convicted, for the use of such person or persons as
the same is hereby appointed to be forfeited and paid unto, and in default thereof, shall be committed by such
justice or justices to the house of correction for any
time not exceeding six months, unless the money forfeited shall be sooner paid.

"Provided nevertheless that it shall and may be lawful to and for such owner or owners of the fishery of such
river or stream of water, or of such pond, pool or other
water wherein any such offence or offences last mentioned shall be committed as aforesaid, to sue and pro-
secute for, and recover, the said sum of five pounds by
action of debt, bill, plaint or information, in any of his
Majesty's courts of record at Westminster; and in such
action or suit no essoign wager of law, or more than one
imparlance shall be allowed; provided such action or
suit be brought or commenced within six calendar
months next after such offence or offences shall have
been committed.

"Provided always, and be it further enacted by the
authority aforesaid, that nothing in this act shall extend,
or be construed to extend, to subject or make liable any
person or persons to the penalties of this act who shall
fish, take, or kill and carry away any fish in any river
or stream of water, pond, pool or other water wherein

such person or persons shall have a just right or claim to take, kill, or carry away any such fish.

To preserve the breed of fish.

There are several acts of parliament to preserve fish and fisheries, by penalties and punishments for using certain nets, and taking fish under a proper size, and out of season, from which the following quotations are made. The first worthy of notice, I believe, is an act passed in the thirteenth year of Richard II, which says,

"No persons shall put in the waters of Thamise, Humber, Ouze, Trent, nor any other waters in any time of the year, any nets called stalkers, nor other nets or engines by which the fry or breed of Salmon, Lampreys, or any other fish may in any wise be taken or destroyed; and the waters of Lon, Wyre, Mersey, Ribble, and all other waters in Lancashire, shall be put in defence, as to taking of Salmon from Michaelmas to Candlemas, and in no other time of the year."

By an act made in the seventeenth year of the same reign,

"The justices of the peace and the mayor of London, on the Thames and Medway, shall survey the offences in both the acts above mentioned, and shall survey and search all the wears in such rivers, that they shall not be very strait for the destruction of such fry and brood, but of reasonable wideness, after the old assize used or accustomed; and they shall appoint under-conservators, who shall be sworn to make the

like survey, search and punishment: and they shall en-
quire in sessions, as well by their office as at the information of the under-conservators, of all defaults aforesaid, and shall cause them which shall be thereof indicted, to come before them, and if they thereof be
convicted, they shall have imprisonment, and make
fine, at the discretion of the justices; and if the same
be at the information of an under-conservator, he shall
have half the fine."

And by a later act,

"No person shall take, or knowingly have in his
possession, either in water or on shore, or sell or ex-
pose to sale, any spawn, fry or brood of fish, or any
unsizeable fish, or fish out of season, or any Smelt not
five inches long; and any person may seize the same,
together with the baskets and package, and charge a
constable or other peace officer with the offender, and
with the goods, who shall carry them before a justice,
the same shall be forfeited and delivered to the prosecutor, and the offender shall besides forfeit twenty shillings, to be levied by distress by warrant of such justice, and distributed, half to the prosecutor, and half
to the poor of the parish where the offence was committed, (and any inhabitant of such parish may nevertheless be a witness) and for want of sufficient
distress, to be committed to the house of correction, to
be kept to hard labour for any time not exceeding three
months, unless the forfeiture be sooner paid, provided
the justice may mitigate the said penalty, so as not to
remit above one half: persons aggrieved may appeal to
the next sessions."

And an old act of parliament of Henry II, says,

"No person shall fasten any nets over rivers, to stand continually night and day, on pain of forfeiting one hundred shillings to the King."

APPENDIX.

HINTS TO YOUNG ANGLERS; WITH DIRECTIONS FOR MAKING GROUND-BAITS, &c.

DURING the winter quarter the angler must not expect many days, or even hours, when he can indulge in his favourite amusement; for the pinching frost which binds up every water in icy chains, is scarcely less favourable than the boisterous winds and heavy rains, which cause the rivers to overflow and inundate the low lands around them, and not only disturb and discolour the waters, but even render them, in many cases, inaccessible. This, therefore, is the proper time for the angler to examine his tackle, and repair whatever is amiss; to see whether his stock of the various articles requisite is complete, and if not, to add to it whatever is wanting. The rods should be now examined, and repaired if any repairs are wanting, and above all, new varnishing should be done at this season; and, by the way, let me advise my angling friends to be particular in scraping off the old varnish before they put on new, or if they even send their rods from home to be re-varnished, let them take the trouble to scrape off the old themselves. Nothing should be omitted on the part of the angler to make his apparatus as complete as possible, that he may not be employed in making or repairing tackle at a season when his time might be better employed in using it. Gay has given the fisherman some wholesome advice on this subject in the following beautiful lines, in the first canto of his Rural Sports:

> When genial Spring a living warmth bestows,
> And o'er the year her verdant mantle throws,
> No swelling inundation hides the grounds,
> But chrystal currents glide within their bounds:
> The finny brood their wonted haunts forsake,
> Float in the sun, and skim along the lake;
> With frequent leap they range the shallow streams,
> Their silver coats reflect the dazzling beams.
> Now let the fisherman his toils prepare,
> And arm himself with every watery snare;
> His hooks, his lines, peruse with careful eye,
> Increase his tackle, and his rod re-tie.

My advice, however, is to prepare every thing needful while—

> The swelling inundation hides the ground,

and not have it to do—

> When genial Spring a living warmth bestows.

Ground-baiting is but little practised by inexperienced anglers; it is also sometimes neglected by the more experienced, from the hurry to begin their sport, or the dislike of the trouble of preparing it: let the neglect arise from what cause it may, little success will attend their efforts in bottom or float-fishing without it, for ground-baiting is an essential in angling. I shall therefore give ample directions how to make and apply every kind useful to promote the angler's sport, as it is necessary that he should first be acquainted with the means of drawing the fish together, before he attempts to take them.

GROUND-BAIT FOR ROACH, DACE, AND BLEAK.

The most simple ground-bait is made by moulding or working some clay (which is generally met with in the banks of rivers) and bran together, into balls or pieces about the size of a pigeon's egg: some add a little bread crumbled among it. This is good ground-bait for Roach and Dace: if you fish in a stream, always put a small stone in each piece before you cast into the water, to prevent it from drifting away.

GROUND-BAIT MADE OF BREAD, BRAN, POLLARD, &c. FOR CHUB, CARP, ROACH, AND DACE.

For a day's angling, half a quartern loaf is necessary, the crust of which you will cut off, the crumb to be cut in slices about two inches thick, and put into a pan, or some deep vessel, and covered with water; when the bread is quite soaked or saturated, squeeze it nearly dry, then add the bran and pollard by handfulls, equal quantities of each, and kneed them together, similar to making bread, until the whole is nearly as stiff as clay: in making this ground-bait, it requires some labour and time, but it will amply repay you for the trouble, as it is the best and cleanest ground-bait for Carp, Chub, Roach and Dace. When I use it for Barbel, in the river Lea, I first break about a quarter of a pound of greaves with a hammer, almost to dust, and soak it well in water, then work it up with the bread, bran, and pollard. In using this bait, you avoid the dirty use of clay, and can also prepare it before you leave home: an equally good bait may be made by substituting barley-meal for the bran and pollard. This should only be used in still water, as from its lightness, it would be carried away in a rapid stream.

GROUND-BAIT MADE WITH CLAY, BRAN AND GENTLES, FOR CHUB, ROACH, AND CARP.

Mix the bran and clay together in lumps about the size of an apple, put a dozen or more gentles in the middle, and close the clay over them similar to making a dumpling; this ground-bait is very enticing to Carp, Chub, Roach and Dace; it is particularly well calculated for baiting in a pond, a still hole, or gentle eddy, because the clay lies at the bottom, and the gentles gradually work through it, which keeps the fish about the hook, and they doubtless mistake your bait on it for what may have escaped from the lump.

GROUND-BAIT MADE WITH CLAY AND GREAVES, FOR BARBEL.

According to the strength of the stream proportion the size of the lumps or balls you cast into the water; in the river Thames, when fishing for Barbel in a punt, the balls must be as large as a turnip, or the current washes them from the places you intend enticing the fish to; in the river Lea, pieces of half the size will do. To make this groundbait, chop or break a pound of greaves into smaller pieces, and cover it with hot water; let it remain until it softens, then pour the water from it and pick out a sufficient quantity of the white pieces to bait your hook, and work up the remainder with clay into lumps or balls; I always add bran to it. This is the best ground-bait for Barbel that is used; it is a considerable time before it parts or dissolves, and keeps the fish to the spot, who rout and push it about with their noses, and occasionally loosen small pieces of the greaves, of which they are immoderately fond: it is also an excellent bait for Chub; large Dace and heavy Roach will also feed on greaves.

GENTLES AND WORMS USED AS GROUND-BAIT FOR CARP, TENCH, ROACH, DACE, &c.

In ponds and in deep still holes gentles may be thrown in by handfulls, to entice fish; but it does not answer in a current or stream, as they then float, and are carried from the spot you intend to angle in: a few mixed with bran and clay will answer better than handfulls without.

If you intend using gentles alone for ground-bait, it will be necessary to take a quart for a day's fishing: gentles for this purpose are called carrion gentles, and are sold at four-pence and six-pence per quart, by Mrs. Embry, fishing-tackle maker, Union-Street, Bishopsgate-Street, Mr. Webster, Grub-Street, and Mr. Rastall, No. 8, Sleep's-Alley, at the top of St. John's-Street, Clerkenwell. Worms cut in pieces may be used with the same precaution in respect to the stream, for ground-bait; if mixed with bran and clay it will be better.

Grains are good ground-bait for Carp, Tench and Eels, in ponds or still waters; but they must be quite fresh, for if they are the least sour, the fish will not come near them. This ground-bait should be thrown in the night before you intend to fish; the same method should be observed when you ground-bait with worms: coarse ground-bait may be made with clay, soaked greaves, and oat chaff; some anglers prefer this to any other for Barbel and Chub.

OBSERVATIONS ON POND-FISHING.

Angling for fish in ponds is more fit for the inexperienced or novice in angling, than in rivers or swift streams, for generally speaking, fish in ponds and still waters are not so large, strong, active or well-fed, as fish are in rivers; they are therefore, more easily allured and taken by a baited hook, neither is it of such material consequence to provide such fine or superior tackle, to plumb the depth so accurately, or to throw so much of choice ground-bait in; for fish in ponds and confined waters, have not such a variety or quantity of food, as is produced or found in rivers and streams; indeed some ponds are so over-stocked with fish, that those which are taken are generally very thin, ill-shaped and coloured, and half-starved, particularly if there has been a long drought, the springs are then very low, and the water in ponds the same: at such times fish will take almost any bait that is offered. From these causes it is apparent, that ponds or still water fishing is best calculated for those who have had little or no practice in the art of angling, as less skill, application, or labour is required, than in rivers.—Note. Fish do not feed so much on the ground in ponds as in rivers.

AN EXPLANATION

OF

TECHNICAL TERMS

USED IN ANGLING.

To *angle*, to catch fish with a rod and line.

Bank-fishing, angling from a bank on the side of a river, or other water.

Beard, or *harb*, of a hook, is that part a little above the point, which prevents the fish slipping off.

Bobber, or *brother bob*, nick-names for anglers.

Bottom-fishing, angling with any bait under water.

Dopping, or *dipping*, falling gently into the water.

Deeps are the deepest parts of the river Thames somewhat out of the current: to make them safe harbours for fish to breed in, &c. the boatmen who live at Hampton, Shepperton, and other places in that neighbourhood, sink their old boats in rows, leaving a channel between them; in a line with this channel they fix their boats when engaged by anglers. The largest Barbel and other fish are taken in these *deeps*, for the manner in which the boats are sunk, effectually protects them from every kind of net.

Drag, a piece of iron wire with four hooks, (without barbs) placed back to back, to which is fastened a long packthread line: this is used to recover any part of the tackle that may be entangled in weeds, &c.

Disgorger, an instrument with a forked top, about six inches long, made of bone, iron or brass: when the fish has swallowed the hook, the forked end of the *disgorger* is thrust upon it, which disengages it, and permits it to be easily drawn out.

Eddies are bends or corners in rivers, where the water meets with obstruction, causing it to recoil and whirl round· fish lie much in these spots, as the motion of the water frequently brings food out of the stream and gives it a momentary pause.

To feed: fish are said to *feed* when they take the bait.

Gentles are maggots bred from fly-blows on liver, or any putrid animal substance.

Gimp, silk twist laced with brass, sold at all fishing-tackle shops.

To *gorge,* to swallow.

Greaves, the sediment of melted tallow; to be bought at the tallow-chandlers.

Ground bait, greaves, bran and clay, gentles, &c. thrown into the water for the purpose of keeping the fish round the spot you intend to angle in.

Heavy fish, large fish.

To *hook foul,* to hook a fish by any part outside its body, which sometimes happens by their swimming against the bait and thereby acting on the float the same as a bite; by striking at the moment, the fish is *hooked foul.* This happens frequently when angling for Barbel.

Killing bait, that bait which the fish are most fond of.

Kink, the line is said to *kink* or *kinkle,* when it gets entangled or twisted about the rod or rings, &c.

Landing-net, a small net extended on an iron hoop, fastened to a pole, which is very useful in landing a large fish, to prevent the straining your rod, &c.

Leather-mouthed fish are those which have their teeth in the throat, as is the case with Barbel, Chub, Carp, &c.

Nibble, the fish are said to *nibble* when they slightly touch the bait, but avoid taking it into the mouth.

Paternoster-line, a line with several hooks, from five to ten or twelve.

To *play a fish,* to let him run a certain distance after having hooked him, then checking him by shortening the line, and again yielding to him, until he is exhausted.

To *pouch,* to swallow.

Prime, fish are said to be *prime* when they rise to the surface, and leap out of the water: when they do this the angler considers it a good sign, as they are then on the feed.

Punt, a broad flat-bottomed boat large enough to hold two or three chairs; it is used in angling on the river Thames, at Richmond, Twickenham, Kingston, Hampton, &c.

Rise, the fish are said to *rise* when they come to the surface to take a fly or any other insect.

A *run,* (in trolling) a bite.

Running-tackle, the line is so called when passed from a winch fixed on the rod, through rings, to join the baited line.

Scowers are places in rivers with a clean sandy or gravelly bottom, on which the fish feed, rub and roll themselves just before they spawn; and many continue on the *scowers* during the warm or hot months.

To *scower worms,* to free them from filth, and make them transparent, by putting them in damp moss, &c.

Shank of a hook, that part to which the line is tied.

Strike, striking a fish is done by giving a sudden jerk from the wrist or arm, when the fish has taken the bait.

Swims, are deep places in rivers where the stream is not rapid: fish are mostly found in them in cool weather.

To *take* or *kill fish*, to catch fish: the words catch and caught are seldom used by anglers.

Trolling, angling with a small fish (either dead or alive) for a bait. This word is derived from the French word *troller*, to stroll or rove about.

Tumbling-bay is a pool of considerable depth and breadth, receiving the surplus water which falls from the flood-gates erected in rivers and canals to keep up a head of water: they are numerous in the river Lea.

To *weigh a fish out*, to lift a fish out of the water by the line, without the aid of a landing net.

Winch, a machine made of brass, on which a line is kept, made of India twist, plaited silk, or gut and silk twisted.

Finis.

CARPENTER & SON, Engravers and Printers,
Aldgate High-Street.